CATALYSTS FOR HOPE

UNLOCKING ENERGY, OPTIMISM, AND YOUR
FULL POTENTIAL

THANE MARCUS RINGLER

Copyright © 2020 by Thane Marcus Ringler

All rights reserved.

No part of this book may be reproduced in any form or by any electronic or mechanical means, including information storage and retrieval systems, without written permission from the author, except for the use of brief quotations in a book review.

To my Dad: the man who has always believed in me and infused hope into everything I've pursued.

INTRODUCTION: UNDERSTANDING HOPE

Ever since I was a little boy, I was tasked with the goal of moving a 1.68-inch white ball into a hole that was, on average, over 400 yards away.

The idea of this task is almost irrational, and certainly illogical. It's hard to fathom accomplishing this goal even with it as is, let alone trying to incorporate 14 club options, different lengths of grass, pits filled with sand, hilly mounds protecting where the hole is located, and the general challenges that all types of inclement weather can bring. Yet, after enough training, practice, failed attempts, and learnings, progress is seen and skill begins to develop.

Then, suddenly, there's a shift... no longer do you just *try* to make contact with the tiny white ball, you are now aiming for making it into the hole in as few of strokes as possible. This transition from trying to make contact, to trying to make a good score is fueled by a small, tiny, source of energy that wells up in the spirit of every golfer alike—*hope*.

Hope is essential to playing golf well (or playing golf at all for that matter). In order to keep coming back to a game that constantly humbles you, like golf, you have to have some semblance of hope that this day will be different, that this day you will have the swing and the shots to post a score you're proud of. That maybe, just maybe, you'll hit that perfect shot keeping you coming back itching for more.

Hope

Hope is as essential for the game of golf as it is essential for any athletic endeavor. The great feat of running a four-minute mile would never have been accomplished if there wasn't **hope** saying it was possible—believing that what hasn't been done *could* be done.

The four-minute mile also shows us that hope is most essential (and hardest to hold onto) for those pressing to accomplish the most outlandish or daring endeavors. Yet, this doesn't apply only to record-breakers or global innovators, this directly applies to you and the outlandish or daring pursuits beyond *your* perceived limits. Hope is essential for us all, to push past our limiting beliefs and accomplish what we are created and called to do here on earth.

Hope is needed for so many parts of our daily lives. Whether it be:

— Asking a girl out on a date (the hope she says Yes!)

— Interviewing for a job (the hope that you get said job)

— Working out in the gym (the hope that a beach-bod will appear)

— Writing words down and putting them in a book (the hope that they will make a tangible difference in the reader's life)

— Waking up in the morning (the hope that this day will be different)

Hope is everywhere in our life, so why are we so bad at embracing it?

What Prevents Us From Embracing Hope

For some reason, we seem to be averse to the idea of hope. Even the fact that you're reading this book with a title like "Catalysts For Hope" is a bold move. In our post-modern, western society, we've begun to see hope as some sort of fantasy or a childish idea. It seems outdated to have hope.

Many things can get in the way of us and hope joining forces, but here is shortlist of things I've found that prevent us from having hope:

— Pride

— Cynicism / pessimism

— Past failures / hurts

— Fear

— Depression, anxiety, worries

— Love of comfort, safety, and security

— News outlets that only depict the bad in our world

— Social media that portrays idealistic images and facades

Ultimately, the narrative / stories we tell ourselves.

Hope Isn't By Chance

There are plenty of obstacles that get in the way of us embracing and leaning into the energy-source, the life-source, that hope can be. Hope doesn't happen by chance.

Because of this, understanding the catalysts for hope can give us a clear path forward for making hope a cornerstone of our being. In this short treatise on the matter, I want to share four catalysts for hope (using 4 P's as an alliteration to help us hold onto these reminders).

1. (In) Process

2. Progress

3. Possibility

4. Purpose

Through reminding ourselves of the power found in these four catalysts, I believe we will begin to expand the outer limits of our perceived abilities, while inspiring and encouraging others to do the same. We will begin to live more fully alive, with motivation and inspiration to take on each day, filled with passion and vigor. We will be kinder to ourselves, knowing we are all in-process. We will celebrate our wins, seeing the progress we've made. We will begin believing in the possibility and leaning into what our potential might be. And we will live each day, attached and aligned with our purpose, brimming with hope each step of the way.

I pray these thoughts and musings may bring about even just a microcosm of these fruits in your life, unlocking a fullness never experienced before. God knows the world needs more hope, and you are the key.

1

CATALYST 1: (IN) PROCESS

YOU'RE NOT FINISHED YET

"Only death is static; the principle of life is change, and we have many deaths and rebirths to transit if we are to lead meaningful lives."

— James Hollis

"Living structures can only be if they become; they can exist only if they change. Change and growth are inherent qualities of the life process."

— Erich Fromm

"The good life is a process, not a state of being. It is a direction not a destination."

— Carl Rogers

Benjamin Franklin is said to have coined the infamous phrase about the only two guarantees in life: ____ & ____.

Unless you've been living underground, I'm fairly certain you passed the quiz with flying colors. 1) Death and 2) Taxes seem to be the only two things guaranteed in life.

Of course there are always other arguments made. If you do a simple google search for "guarantees in life," you will find endless articles on an array of opinions regarding what should be added alongside death and taxes. I believe the original deduction by Franklin carries with it the right balance of brevity and truth, making it a fair analysis of the human condition.

Part of the truth that this cliche conveys is that life is filled with movement, dynamism, and change.

Defining Terms

We all love definitions (guilty). Part of this affinity comes from the finality in a definition. It's saying: "this is what the word means, no more questions asked." This definitive state is comforting because it's final... at least that's one point of view.

I believe there is *more* hope found in **description** rather than **definition**, and I also believe that hope is essential if we are to live out "the good life."

It's helpful to start out with the definition of "hope." What Google comes up with is: "a feeling of expectation and desire for a certain thing to happen."

What Thane came up with is: "a resource that is desperately needed for a life well-lived and a race run with endurance."

The main difference between the two is that one is a definition and one is a description. Let's unpack the importance of that difference before we return to hope.

Definitive vs. Descriptive

Martin Luther King Jr. is a modern-day icon and figure of hope. His legacy, inspiration, and impact will continue to live on in-part because he understood this distinction, and the phrase that he is most famously known for reveals this: "I have a dream." If one word was changed, the entire phrase loses the majority of its power and impact.

"I have a dream" — descriptive.

"I had a dream" — definitive.

If MLK used the word "had" instead of "have," he would've been defining a dream he had, not a vision he is carrying forward to empower the American society and future generations to come. Speaking in the past tense would have created a sense of finality to the vision, which I believe would have diminished the power, weight, and trajectory of his actual message.

One word can change the entire message. This is the power of hope and the importance of the distinction between *definitive* and *descriptive*.

There are many layers to this distinction, but most fundamental is the difference between **having arrived** vs. **being in-process**. Defining something shows that you have arrived to a conclusive end-point. Describing something is a way of defining it in terms of how you see it in the moment, leaving room for growth in the future.

In life it is safe to say that we never fully arrive. Arriving is only a temporary and fleeting reality, because destinations always remain in the present moment. Once you reach one, there will inevitably be another to reach (until Franklin's first guarantee, that is). This is why our job is to keep pushing towards the next destination after each momentary arrival.

What is Finished?

There are very few things in life that are ever finished.

Here's a shortlist I came up with of things that are "finished":

- A book: While this is true in part, the larger reality is that once it is published there is finality in its form, but the function of the material will be shifting as our perspectives and thought-process shifts and grows in the future.
- A meal: Hunger will always be a part of the human existence (definitive), but how hungry we are is much more of a descriptive condition.
- A job: But of course there will always be another job to be done
- A war / conflict: Once any conflict is resolved, there are inevitably disputes that await down the road.
- Education: This is really only finished in the formal sense after high-school, college, or grad school, because everything in life is an education.

For me personally, there are other areas that can seem definitive on their surface. Faith, for one, cannot be definitive because that would mean sight, and faith is largely defined as the hope in things unseen/unknown.

Even things such as personality traits—ranging from the introverted to extroverted spectrum to the Enneagram and other personality assessments—are more-so descriptions of your natural disposition rather than definitions of who you are. Again, this is a very important distinction because one side tends to put us in a box closing the lid, whereas the other side provides structure to help process while still allowing us the freedom to move around or even jump into a different framework beside or beyond.

Seasons are another great example of the power of descriptions instead of definitions. When we are in a low-season—a season of discouragement, trial, or hardship—thinking of it as a definitive state would fill us with helplessness and despair.

Understanding that a season is descriptive of the now but not definitive of the future helps us use that season for good while maintaining an expectation of what's ahead.

Where it Shows Up In Life

When I first became aware of this distinction, it intrigued me but I didn't fully understand its significance. After becoming more aware of its presence, through conversations with others and reflection paired with contemplation in my own life, I've begun to see how pervasive this distinction really is.

One of the most prevalent places this can show up is in the thought-pattern that says: "once I get to ____, or once I complete ____, then I'll be ____." This is the false assumption of a final arrival in life, one of the core dangers in definitive thinking. The final arrival will never happen in this life, which is why this definitive thought-pattern results in a lack of fulfillment, stemming largely from *false expectations*.

Honestly this can show up anywhere and everywhere. It comes from our natural disposition to desire the definite, to be able to categorize every aspect of our daily lives. This is a much easier path in the short-run, giving finality and closure to an area of life or thought, but in the long-run it limits both our growth and our potential. This is also described as the "fixed vs. growth mindset."

Having a definitive posture vs. a descriptive posture leads to closed-mindedness instead of open-mindedness. By embracing descriptive thinking, we are able to recognize and categorize the things we learn and experience in life, while affording that experience-based knowledge the freedom to shift and morph as we grow throughout our lives.

What Can This Unlock?

I believe there are five main benefits this distinction can unlock in our lives:

(1) PRESENCE - in being fully here in the moment, appreciating it for what it is, and being grateful for where we are in the process.

(2) FUEL - by helping us know we haven't arrived, there's still work to be done, growth is always possible, and there is no limit for better.

(3) ENCOURAGEMENT - not just for ourselves, but for others in our lives; helping them see their own potential and understand what is descriptive rather than definitive.

(4) GRACE - helping us give grace to others, but more importantly to ourselves! Knowing that we are, and always will be, in-process helps us show more love and be kinder to ourselves in the journey we're on (something I'm often quite bad at).

(5) POTENTIAL - ultimately unlocking our fullest and truest potential.

If I could summarize all these words into one hope-filled phrase, it would be this quote by Diego Simila:

"Forward progress is not a finished process."

This is hope.

This is fuel for life.

This is being human.

LIFE IS HARD, which is why hope is needed.

Next time you feel the urge to define, allow yourself a moment to pause, to find hope in the process you are in—knowing that forward progress is never a finished process.

One Caveat

There is one final caveat I must add. I believe the one thing in life that never changes is God — the Creator and Sustainer of all of life — and who He is is both definitive and descriptive. Definitive in the sense that He never changes and will always and forever be the great I AM (Hebrews 13:8) Yet, He is also descriptive in that He meets us where we are and how we need it in the specific moment we are in.

As a Christ-follower, my ultimate hope in life is found in the person of Jesus Christ — the Son of God. He is the "sure and steadfast anchor for the soul" the hope I hold fast to in the midst of life's storms (Hebrews 6).

And the beauty of knowing Him is… God's not finished with you yet.

Praise God for promised growth, promised progress, the reminder of life never being a finished-process.

2

CATALYST 2: PROGRESS

WHY THE LITTLE THINGS ARE THE BIG THINGS

"The man who moves a mountain begins by carrying away small stones."

— Confucius

"The most important shot in golf is the next one."

— Ben Hogan

Every step matters.

One of the best books I read in 2018 was Steven Johnson's *How We Got To Now*. One of the common themes throughout his book was the necessity of multiple innovations to finally arrive at the innovation we use today. One example that stuck with me was the creation of devices to record and project what we hear—aka: audio devices.

While most people recognize Thomas Edison as the one who

pioneered the ability to record and play back audio through the phonograph, this giant, innovative leap was only made possible by the first leap made twenty years prior: the invention of the phonoautograph. Edouard-Leon Scott de Martinville (what a name) invented the phonoautograph in 1857 as a way to record the sound waves as they passed through air. In his mind, the next logical step would be to create a new language around reading and deciphering the sound waves that were transmuted into lines on paper (earliest form of transcription, albeit not very helpful when it appears as scribbled lines instead of legible letters).

In hindsight, the obvious innovation is to use those waves to actually recreate and play the sound back, but at the time, this next step was not so obvious at all. Yet, without this first innovative leap, Edison may have never been able to make the consequential, giant leap in creating the phonograph that both records and plays back the audio sounds. Each innovative step forward is crucial for facilitating the innovation that's yet to come. Shortcuts simply aren't an option.

The point of this example is to illustrate that the little steps add up to the big steps. The next step is better than skipping to step ten, because skipping to step ten usually doesn't last without the first nine steps it took to get there, often because the problem we're trying to solve isn't the real problem. It takes learning what the problem *isn't* in order to learn what the problem *is*.

A necessary part of growth is first learning what NOT to do before we learn what TO do.

Each and every step matters.

From Belief To Action

The first catalyst for hope was all about the foundational hope of knowing we are never finished in life—or stated in the affirmative: **we are always in-process**. Which means, our current place in life is more *descriptive* than it is *definitive*. It means that growth is possible, whether or not it looks like the picture of growth we imagined.

In this second part, my goal is to discuss what our focus in that process should be—how we can leverage hope to our advantage and add fuel to fan the flame to higher and higher realms.

If knowing that growth is always possible is the first step to living a hope-filled life, then the second step is to believe that hope by acting on it, by taking the steps forward proving that belief.

"We only know what we act on. We only believe what we obey."

— James Sire

Steps Are Smaller Than You Think

If the first reminder we need to preach to ourselves is that every step matters, the second reminder is that *most steps are smaller than we think*.

They say a picture is worth a thousand words; I'd say that's a gross understatement. A thousand words can often be pretty cheap (like a chapter in this book), but a picture of beauty only comes from great effort and exertion over a long period of time. It's a journey, and a journey entails a lot of steps.

> "The journey of a thousand miles begins with a single step."
>
> — Lao Tzu

Just as every journey begins with a single step, every journey ends with a single step, and between those two points are a whole heck of a lot more steps than any of us ever want to admit. In fact, a thousand miles is roughly equivalent to two million steps... *two million*. Whatever your "thousand mile journey" is in life right now, the irrefutable aspect of that journey is: it will entail countless steps. Steps that, by themselves, seem meaningless, but when they are stacked on top of each other they can add up to incredible destinations.

> "Celebrating small steps triggers more dopamine than saving it all up for one big achievement."
>
> — Loretta Graziano Breuning

The important, objective reality about steps is: they don't *just happen*.

Steps require ***effort + intention***.

Just because we are in-process doesn't mean there is a *guarantee* of progress. In fact, without intention paired with exertion there will be little chance of growth. Decay is the natural order of the world. Entropy happens by chance, growth does not. Growth takes effort... but typically it isn't some herculean-effort that's required.

Part of the beauty found in hope is that it has large implications. Hope can move mountains and withstand any onslaught from the fiercest of storms. Yet, the fruit from this hope isn't often a magnificent, grandiose accomplishment or feat. Rather, it is the small, microscopic, yet doggedly-persistent movement in the direction of progress. The clawing your way forward, inching along the ground in ways that seem slower than a sloth but still amount to some measure of "forward." This is the more common reality of hope, and it is exactly why the little things are the big things.

Any big leap is facilitated by the countless little steps that created the result of a "big leap." We all love to glorify the major innovation at the expense of all the innocent, seemingly invisible, baby steps that did all of the dirty work needed to arrive at the deified destination. But as we all know, the journey is the destination, it's just not as sexy or novel.

Hope does not depend on novelty.

Hope depends on conviction.

Hope involves faith.

So, if each step matters, and if those steps are usually smaller than bigger, how does that correlate with hope and progress?

Fueling Hope

Hope and progress are related because hope provides the fuel for consistent and continual progress in life, especially when our feelings or emotions are saying otherwise.

So, if hope is fuel for progress, what is the fuel for hope?

As with tending a good fire, knowing the things that will help our hope remain ablaze is important. Here is a shortlist of hope-fuel from my experience:

— **Progress**: seeing tangible signs of ground gained helps hope grow into an even stronger resource.

— **Promises**: hearing the promised outcome of any effort brings a greater conviction to the effort that awaits.

— **Community**: surrounding yourself with others who share the hope you hold will increase your own resiliency and support you in the valleys.

— **Reminders**: reflecting on your own experiences that have reenforced hope, as well as the lessons of history and others' lives can all be important fuel for sustained hope.

— **Experiences**: experiencing progress, the fruit of that hope, is undeniable personal evidence that can't be refuted, even in the wake of the strongest emotions or opposition.

— **Inspiration**: seeing the example of others' accomplishments and achievements can add to our own hope as we see what's possible from our fellow humans.

— **Positive impact on others**: seeing the fruit of your influence, impact, or support on others' lives helps add further fuel to the work at hand.

— **Challenge**: having the right threshold of challenge, a goal that's sufficiently beyond your current reach but not too far to be seemingly out of grasp, is a hope-inducing sweet-spot.

— **Competition**: healthy competition is one of the most consistent fuel sources for hope; it is often in ready supply and it can bring a human element that incorporates many of the aforementioned fuels as well.

Hope Extinguishers

Just as important as knowing what sustains a fire, we must be aware of the elements that can extinguish our hope-flame. Hope has many opponents, but here are few from my experience:

Slow Progress

The slower the growth, the more frustrating the process can become. One of the most difficult parts of reaching a level of mastery in golf was the fact that progress became so incremental. Hours and hours of practice would hardly produce anything more than microscopic improvements.

Doubt

Doubt is the opposite of faith and a it is direct opponent to hope. The more we entertain (or give mental space) to doubts, the more hope's flame will be reduced to a flicker.

Fear

Fear is the opposite of freedom, and living in fear stifles hope until it has no air to breath. When we are operating from a fear-based mindset, we tend to only focus on worst-case scenarios, not on the hope that is propelling our actions.

Wrong Focus

Something as innocent as a misdirected focus can also hurt hope's flame. A focus on responsibilities and duties instead of opportunities can transform hope into a burden instead of a blessing.

Others' Opinions

If we allow our hope to be based on what other people think or believe then our flame is sure to dwindle. Everyone has an opinion, and most everyone's opinion will differ. Sustainable fuel is found when your hope is not based on others' and their opinions.

Lethargy / Laziness

Defaulting to laziness and settling for less than we are capable of will naturally lead to a reduction in hope's flame. Action is what fuels belief, inaction will only diminish our hope until the flame is extinguished.

Too Hard of a Challenge

Having a challenge or goal that is beyond the healthy sweet-spot will often lead to despair. Knowing the difference between what seems impossible and what truly is impossible is important to discern in order to keep hope's flame burning strong.

Too Much Competition

An abundance of competition can lead to burnout or, even worse, complete loss of hope. Know what level of competition is helpful rather than hurtful to ensure hope's flame doesn't get snuffed out.

> "Action feeds and strengthens confidence; inaction in all forms feeds fear. To fight fear, act. To increase fear—wait, put off, postpone."
>
> — David Schwartz

Summation

To summarize, the simplest way to live a life committed to progress and hope is to understand and believe that the small steps are the big steps—embracing baby steps as the necessary route to greatness.

How do we live lives of hope?

1. Live for something beyond yourself.
2. Live attached to that vision — *daily*.
3. Use the hope-fuel to increase the flame and keep the fire burning hot.
4. Be aware of the elements in life that look to extinguish hope.

As my former training group poignantly coined: **Everything is everything**.

The little things are the big things.

Baby steps matter, and progress is the fuel that hope needs — no matter how small it might seem.

"What we call the beginning is often the end

And to make an end is to make a beginning.

The end is where we start from."

— T.S. Elliot

3

CATALYST 3: POSSIBILITY

LEANING INTO THE POTENTIAL

"Some things have to be believed to be seen."

— Madeleine L'Engle

"Capacity is a state of mind. How much we can do depends on how much we think we can do."

— David Schwartz

"So you're saying there's a chance!"

If you're from the same era as me and are at all familiar with the Jim Carrey of old, this phrase brings one particular scene to mind: Lloyd Christmas asking Mary Swanson what his odds are for ending up with her. Standing there in the hotel lobby after a long, arduous, and near-frozen trip to Aspen, Lloyd represents a picture of hope in the middle of what seems to be hopelessness, the one-in-a-million chance of (in Lloyd's words): "a guy like you and a girl like me ending up together" … this is the power of possibility, and the beauty of hope.

In a less Hollywood-esque example, possibility has played an active role in every golf shot I've ever consciously hit. During a recent a trip to the practice green, I realized how large of a role this idea actually represents. Even from a single practice session, chipping and putting around the green, the implications were crystal clear. When I came into a chip or a putt with a vision for the possibility of hitting a good shot, that good shot came into being a majority of the time. This "hack" almost feels like a cheat-code you would use in a video game, it's that freakishly connected.

In life, this is more true than we often want to admit or believe, because once we believe it then we have no other option than to take action.

What Are Possibilities?

Thane's definition of possibility is: "the stimulant that helps us lean into our full potential and embrace our calling in this beautiful adventure called life." Ultimately, this means both *leaning into* and *living in* the possibility of what lies ahead.

If leaning into and living in the possibility allows us to express our full potential while living lives characterized by hope, then what are these possibilities?

Possibilities can be many things:

— Possibilities are unconfined

— Possibilities are future oriented

— Possibilities stem from reality

— Possibilities are generative

— Possibilities are contingent (on belief)

— Possibilities are endless

"Reality is a cloud of possibility, not a point."

— Amos Tversky

A possibility can be something similar to Lloyd and Mary ending up together (one-in-a-million) or something similar to me eating some dark chocolate in the evening time (one-in-an-every-other-day). It is a term and an idea that covers a wide span of reality, but it always plays a role regardless of the size of probability at play.

Important Distinctions

A crucial component within the idea of possibility is the difference between a *possibility* and a *probability*. One involves the head, the other focuses on the heart. One hedges bets while the other chooses to go all in.

A possibility does not stem from a probability, but rather from a potential capability.

Possibility utilizes our imagination; probability primarily relies on reflection. One is looking into the future, the other is focusing on the past. Both can be helpful, but one is far more powerful.

"Imagination allows us to conceive of delightful future possibilities, pick the most amazing one, and pull the present forward to meet it."

— Jason Silva

Before we get too lost in the clouds, I do want to mention one other distinction that is important to understand: the difference between *improbable* and *impossible*; the difference between something that seems impossible and something that actually is impossible.

Belief and possibility do have limits, specifically relating to the natural limitations of being human. Some of our human limitations are already known, some are still being discovered and disproved. An example of this distinction is comparing the belief in a human's ability to fly with the belief in a human's ability to run a four-minute mile. One is physically impossible (without technological add-ons), and one was perceived to be impossible until it was famously disproven otherwise.

This fine line is often hard to distinguish.

> "Persistent people are able to visualize the idea of light at the end of the tunnel when others can't see it. At the same time, the smartest people are realistic about not imagining light when there isn't any."
>
> — Seth Godin

What's impossible versus what's improbable can be one of the hardest distinctions to discern, because the improbable almost always seems impossible, regardless of whether it truly is or not. One helpful question to ask when facing this dilemma is whether the possibility you are leaning into feels impossible for the entire human race, or if it just seems impossible for you. If it is a personal impossibility, then it will more likely fall into the improbable column.

Why The "Lean" Matters

As mentioned earlier, my thesis is based on two main objectives: **1) living in**, and **2) leaning into**. Living in means we are remaining in a place of possibility, not settling for less than we are capable of. Leaning into means we are consistently pushing into greater expansions of that possibility as we continue growing personally.

"Leaning in" is an important part of this entire equation because it denotes an active reliance upon the unknown, the potential you possess that lies beyond your current or perceived grasp.

Leaning in always creates some measure of discomfort. One physical illustration of this comes even in human interactions or conversations with others. Leaning in places you into the personal space of the other, often creating a slight discomfort that adds an element of importance, intimacy, or intensity often used in non-verbal communication.

It's important for us to understand this is always harder than easier. Leaning in is scary, vulnerable, and filled with tension. We can often be creatures of comfort, but a life of leaning is a non-stagnant reality requiring a greater dependence on faith, on a belief in a reality not yet seen.

"If you limit yourself only to what seems possible or reasonable, you disconnect yourself from what you truly want, and all that is left is compromise."

— Anaïs Nin

As a Christian, I believe this is God's design, and living by faith is what produces our best life for the world's greatest good, and ultimately God's glory.

Possibility Works Both Ways

There was another layer I observed during the practice session on the golf course. Possibility doesn't just work for creating the ideal shot and outcome I desire, it can just as easily work in producing the negative outcome I fear.

Fear is the default mindset we tend to carry, partly because it is the most pragmatic. It is usually the most believable outcome.

When I'm hitting chips and I hit a poor shot (which happens rather often in golf), the default image in my mind for the next shot will be the negative outcome and the bad chip that just happened. With this on the forefront of my mind, the possibility of hitting another shot like it is amplified ten-fold. This is why negative affirmations tend to produce negative results. When I approach a shot with the mental-chatter saying: "don't hit the ball here", or "don't swing the club this way", I'll end up producing the very thing I told myself not to. This is the power of possibility flipped on its head.

Possibility is a powerful mindset, but it can be more easily used to produce a negative outcome than a positive one.

There's another prominent way this shows up on the golf course. When I've been playing exceptionally well and am in the second half of my round, there is a sneaky tendency to start entertaining the possibility of "messing up." The second I begin to start playing out of fear, from the negative affirmation of trying "not to mess up the good round I have going," is the second I begin to create the fear-driven reality by leaning into the negative possibility.

The bottom line is, possibility will be at work, one way or another. Not sure about you, but I'd much rather have it be used for good instead of creating the reality I dread.

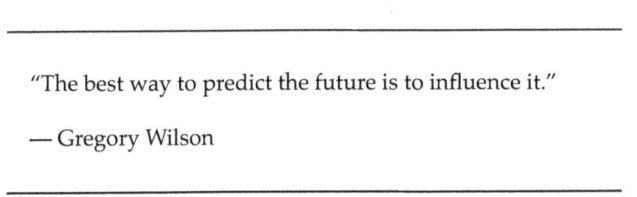

"The best way to predict the future is to influence it."

— Gregory Wilson

Possibility Works In Many Ways

Not only is possibility effective in both positive and negative beliefs, it can also be helpful in different phases of growth and work.

As humans, we have two main functions in life: 1) **creating**, and 2) **cultivating** (idea-credit goes to Andy Crouch in his book: *Culture Making*).

In the creation phase, possibility is crucial because we have to believe it is possible to bring something into existence. But in the cultivation phase, possibility flip flops into a different role. For us to embrace our job as cultivators—maintaining what has been created—we have to believe in the possibility that something can be removed from existence if there is personal negligence. This gives us the motivation to work diligently to cultivate what has been created, knowing that there is a very real possibility of it diminishing or extinguishing entirely without the maintenance and stewardship of that creation.

These are just a few examples of the ways that possibility plays a factor in our daily lives. It can make an impact on every type of work and any type of person. This goes back to the cliche that: *anything is possible*... especially when it comes to possibility.

How To Live In The Possibility

Possibility is such a blessing and an important catalyst to help us have hope in life. It provides purpose by giving us an image or idea to lean into and pursue. And it is a useful tool, both as creators and cultivators of culture and life.

We must always remember that, whether or not something is "possible" depends largely on our belief in the possibility. In everyday life this is more true than we would like to admit, because if we admitted to its power we would then be forced to start taking ownership of that belief. It means we must begin to lean into and live in the possibility of everyday life: of the dreams we are pursuing, of the work we are doing, and of the growth we are experiencing.

Like much of life, possibility is grey—it's not black and white. This means: what's possible is often situational and variable in nature (not stagnant). We can either run away from this tension, or choose to embrace the discomfort of the unknown and make it our home.

There are two final exhortations to be made:

1. Take Ownership

It is ultimately up to us and our belief in our own potential, our belief in the possibility of what's to come, and the opportunities we can create and cultivate in our lives. This is a daily battle we must all fight, but it's a fight that's worth the effort because it's the battle that unlocks our truest potential for the world's greatest good.

2. More Is Possible Than You Expect

We are chronic under-believers in possibility. In daily life, we are not trying to believe in the possibility of flying (obviously impossible), but rather in the possibility of staying focused for an hour time-block to make sure this chapter gets written. Believing in the possibility of a successful sales call. Believing in the possibility of lifting that bar with more weight on it than you've ever lifted before. Believing in the possibility of that girl saying "yes" to a coffee date. Believing in the possibility of benefiting from reading that book instead of watching that show. Believing in the possibility of showing up and working hard, every single day, over a long period of time, as the recipe for reaching the goals set before you.

"Hope is a revolutionary patience. It begins in the dark, the stubborn hope that if you just show up and try to do the right thing, the dawn will come. You wait and watch and work; you don't give up."

— Anne Lamott

Living In The Possibility

Living in the possibility leads to a life of discovery.

Living in the possibility means we believe in our full potential and lean into the discomfort.

Living in the possibility requires us to trust the process of growth and live in the unknown.

Living in the possibility requires us to lean in.

Living in the possibility produces *hope*.

The only question that remains is ... **What's possible?**

... you already know what I would say.

"When I let go of what I am, I become what I might be."

— Lao Tzu

4

CATALYST 4: PURPOSE
LIVING ATTACHED AND ALIGNED

"Don't ask what the world needs. Ask what makes you come alive, and go do it. Because what the world needs is people who have come alive."

— Howard Thurman

"A goal is an objective, a purpose. A goal is more than a dream; it's a dream being acted upon."

— David Schwartz

"He who has a why to live for can bear with almost any how."

— Viktor Frankl

Have you heard of logotherapy?

In today's day and age, we are quick to assume that "Life Coaching" is a modern-day construct, when in reality this has been a part of the 21st century for longer than most assume.

Logotherapy is an applied therapy where the psychologist "assists the client in detecting their specific and individual meaning" [in life]. This therapy is based on the philosophical / scientific basis of "Existential Analysis," which basically means an analysis of one's existence given the prerequisites of a self-responsible, self-realized, and humane life.

Logotherapy is the "fancy" study of finding meaning in life, and it is the brain-child of Viktor Frankl (psychiatrist and neurologist who survived the Nazi concentration camps and wrote about it in his famed book: *Man's Search For Meaning*), who was influenced and inspired by the works of both Sigmund Freud and Alfred Adler, two of his predecessors. In logotherapy analysis: "the search for meaning in life is identified as the primary motivational force in human beings."[1]

One of Frankl's most powerful quotes goes like this:

> "Ever more people today have the means to live, but no meaning to live for."

Even with the passing of many decades since that statement, Frankl's words couldn't ring more true today... sounds like we need a little hope.

Waking Up ON MISSION

When we get out of bed we have two choices to make: 1) either make life happen, or 2) let life happen to us. Each day we have the opportunity to discover, understand, and remind ourselves of the point of our life—what we are living for. Not taking advantage of this opportunity will be the default choice if you do not intentionally or consciously make one. This is one of the greatest maladies, highlighted by Frankl's Psychotherapy, that continues to plague our existence, adding to the rise in depression, anxiety, and suicide.[2]

While phones are an easy scapegoat (and rightfully so), I believe this is a surface wound and not the root. At its core, it is a loss of purpose; a loss of clarity in direction and pursuit; a misconstrued focus on image vs. relationship; an emphasis on self-fulfillment through pleasure instead of meaning.

The beauty in this is that each day we have a choice. Every human has the ability to wake up *on mission*. Each individual has the capacity to set a trajectory for their life and pursue it. Each person can intentionally live with a daily drive for a higher purpose—for something bigger than themselves.

Breaking the Cycle

Until we consciously choose to live on-purpose, we will naturally be living for pleasure, survival, and whatever else life brings our way. This is a cycle that will perpetuate until there is a stimulus for change stronger than the resistance opposing that change.

I recently had the chance to mentor formerly incarcerated youth (most times they teach me more than I could ever teach them). These inspiring and powerful humans are fighting a battle much harder than most who are reading this now. In the battle to break the cycle of poverty, discrimination, bad decisions, violence, drug-use, broken families, and beyond, the single greatest ingredient that will generate the endurance needed to make lasting change is… ***purpose***: pushing for the change and striving to break the cycle for something greater than just themselves. Whether it be family, children, or simply self-worth that was never given to them; purpose is the power that can break the chains of generational cycles which seem insurmountable.

"The chains of habit are too weak to be felt until they are too strong to be broken."

— Samuel Johnson

If these men and women, who many times are dealt cards from a deck stacked against them, can choose to live lives of purpose despite the adversity, so can you and I regardless of the circumstances we may find ourselves in.

We all have a cycle to break, it's time we see it, own it, and shatter it with the hammer of purpose.

The Mechanism

There is a very simple mechanism for living a life of purpose: *conscious choice*.

If the goal is to have purpose attached to our daily life, this goal is accomplished by the mechanism of making a conscious choice to live for something beyond our immediate wants and desires—something beyond our *self*.

The reason for this mechanism can be understood through one of my favorite inventions in all of life: sports.

Why are sports so fun, addicting, and all-consuming? There's the physicality, the teamwork, the competitiveness, and the tribal nature it produces; but I would argue it's something even more fundamental.

The reason why we love sports so dearly and are willing to pour incredible amounts of time, energy, effort, and money into these activities is because: ***they have a clear objective, a defined purpose***. Imagine if basketball didn't have a point? March Madness would be chaos without the clear purpose and rules that any sport must have guiding its participants. If I didn't have a compelling reason to hit a little white ball into a small hole in the ground, there is 0% chance I would ever try to accomplish that.

But there is one other ingredient that must be paired with purpose in this mechanism of making a conscious choice. Sports rely not only on a defined purpose or objective, this purpose must be reinforced by infusing it with ***meaning***. Winners get "x", losers get *nothing!* Without meaning behind the game being played, what fun is left in the game?

Sports are microcosms of life. From this view of sports we can see that living a life of purpose is accomplished by: ***making a conscious choice that's aligned with a clear and defined purpose that's been infused (attached) with meaning***.

"Your calling is found where your deep gladness and the world's deep hunger meet."

— Frederick Beuchner

Seeking Wisdom From Children

Children have the propensity to ask a million questions a day, or so it seems. Childlike curiosity is an attribute I'm quite fond of, and one widely seen as a noble pursuit for adults as well.

The simplest (and often most profound) of all questions is: *why?*

The question of "why" is the question of purpose. Why are

you doing what you are doing? A child's #1 question always seeks to understand the purpose, and we adults think growing up means becoming more wise...

Asking "why" is a question that improves with repetition. Usually the first "why" will be answered by some trivial, surface-level reasoning. The second "why" that follows will try to dig down a layer beneath the surface, but it's almost always the third "why" (and beyond) that finally starts to reveal the true purpose found at the core. This holds true in so many instances, and I've personally experienced its power in the Development Coaching work I do.

The question of why highlights another superpower of purpose: *it clarifies.* Stated simply: purpose cuts through the crap, slicing through the noise and distractions of every day life. Noise produces confusion and confusion can lead to aimlessness. In modern-day society, all we typically experience is noise!

If purpose produces clarity, then clarity produces vision. And if clarity produces vision, then vision produces *hope*.

"The difference between noise and music is very simple: music is two sounds related to each other; noise is the same two sounds not related to each other."

— Wynton Marsalis

Purpose has the ability to turn noise into music, to shift chaos into clarity, to transform aimlessness into direction, and to amplify hope through living under a powerful vision and calling.

> "The only thing worse than blindness is having sight but no vision."
>
> — Helen Keller

Living On Purpose

Living lives of purpose never happens by chance. We have a responsibility to constantly be practicing the daily discipline of infusing our lives with purpose. *Life will never automatically attach itself to our purpose.* That is the work we must do on our own.

This will be a daily battle, a daily endeavor, a daily goal that isn't alway reached. But it is a goal that can be accomplished and measured. Here are my two favorite questions for evaluating where we are at:

1. Am I living connected to my purpose? (Attached)
2. Are my actions and my day-to-day life in union with my purpose? (Aligned)

Simply stated: *Am I living attached and aligned to my purpose?*

Until we can honestly answer that question "YES", we will continue to let life happen to us instead of making life happen. At the end of the day, life is a gift. Let's receive it and own it to the fullest, bringing our greatest gift for the world's greatest good.

> "We may spend most of our waking hours advancing our own interests, but we all have the capacity to transcend self-interest and become simply a part of a

whole. It's not just a capacity; it's the portal to many of life's most cherished experiences."

— Jonathan Haidt

---

1. https://www.viktorfrankl.org/logotherapy.html
2. https://www.cbsnews.com/news/suicide-depression-anxiety-mental-health-issues-increase-teens-young-adults/

5

IN CONCLUSION

We all could use a little more hope.

Hope doesn't just happen by chance, and it isn't some fantastical, mythological reality. Hope is real, (semi-)tangible fuel that can carry us through the darkest of lows and push us to the highest of peaks.

In order to use the essential element of hope, we must be aware of the ways we can approach the everyday components of life to bring hope out in flashing colors.

*KNOWING that we are all in-PROCESS allows us to accept where we are while remaining hopeful of where we may reach.

*SEEING the PROGRESS we've made gives us a boost to keep pressing forward toward the hope of who we can still become.

. . .

*Understanding the power of POSSIBILITY helps us tap into the full potential that lies within each our our souls.

*Living on and for PURPOSE brings the rally-cry of hope front and center for each day we are blessed with in this beautiful dance of life.

Some days are better than others, but you can always count on at least one of these catalysts to help realign you with the mountain-moving power of hope that is possible each and every day, no matter how dire the situation may be.

Viktor Frankl, quoted several times in Catalyst 4, who endured one of the hardest experiences known to man, had these words to say about this power:

Everything can be taken from a man but one thing: the last of human freedoms - to choose one's attitude in any given set of circumstances, to choose one's own way.

We have a choice. We have the ability to choose hope. Not only do we have the ability, but I believe we have a *responsibility.*

Viktor went on to say:

Each man is questioned by life; and he can only answer to life by answering for his own life; to life he can only respond by being responsible.

In Conclusion

Let us answer the questions of life with the pursuit of being responsible—response-able, by choosing hope regardless the cost.

AFTERWORD: THE CASE FOR IDEALISM

Defined

Idealism:

> "elevated ideals or conduct; the quality of believing that ideals should be pursued" (Vocabulary.com)

> "The unrealistic belief in or pursuit of perfection." (Oxford Dictionaries)

> "The belief that your ideals can be achieved, often when this does not seem likely to others"

The idea of idealism is a concept discussed by many in a broad swath of cultural spheres and influences, ranging from Forbes, to the NY Times, to Psychology Today (which we will be referencing in a bit). It is a concept that appears nuanced, yet the range of implications can be seen on multiple levels. From politics, to society, to relationships, careers, and beyond, this is a concept that has cascading effects on the general population at large, and my goal is to unpack these effects and show the importance in unlocking its power.

To begin, let's make this personal...

I can often be an extreme idealist. The funny thing about my idealism is: I have an unwavering confidence in my ability but a skeptical uncertainty in others who are overly zealous about themselves (similar to the self-serving bias innate in all of us).

One of the ways this plays out for me is within my inner-dialogue. I recently submitted a self-tape and proposal to give a TED Talk at a nearby TEDx event happening later this year. I had spent several weeks solidifying the concept for the pitch (which is actually closely tied to this concept of idealism), and had finally come to a point of clarity and confidence in what I was presenting. I spent the whole afternoon finalizing my pitch and filming the audition tape I submitted later that evening. I was feeling good...

Fast forward two weeks and I was still waiting for the verdict on whether I made it past the first round or not. My confidence had actually grown in the time of waiting, and I still believed I would get the call-back.

Then the email came...

The submission was denied, and my opportunity was squelched (talk about an anti-climatic illustration). Initially this was surprising, frustrating, and aggravating. *"How could they not have liked my idea? Why didn't they choose it? What was missing? How could I have been more convincing? Was it foolish and naive to even believe I could land a TEDx Talk?"*

The way we react to these types of disappointments tells us a lot about our place on the spectrum from Idealism to Cynicism.

The Question

Before we get to the spectrum, I want to spend a second on the last question that was posed in my mind: Was I being naive, or even worse, was I being foolish in believing I could give a TEDx Talk?

I firmly hold the conviction that it was neither naive nor foolish, but rather: idealistic… and ultimately: positive and beneficial. Regardless of what you may think while reading this, or what the Speaker Selection Panel thought in rejecting my submission, that doesn't change my self-assessment.

Does that mean I deserved to give a TEDx Talk? Well, apparently not because it didn't happen. But that's not the point. And this gets us back to the spectrum…

The Spectrum

In the realm of idealism, there is a spectrum that ranges from idealism on the positive extreme to cynicism on the negative side. In the middle lies realism—another important concept in understanding how to live a balanced yet impactful life.

I do believe that we are born with and genetically wired to fall on different places within this spectrum. Alongside innate characteristics there are the life experiences that vastly impact our view of the world—nature and nurture as they say. Both are powerful forces in shaping our lives and our outlooks.

To speak to my own experience, I feel I have been blessed in greater proportion than most. I would agree wholeheartedly with Bill Simon when he said: "I was born on third-base and thought I had hit a triple." I can't change the reality I was born into, I can only control how I use what I've been given (which is why we emphasize "being faithful" so much on our podcast - The Up & Comers Show). Due to being born into an upper-class family as a caucasian male who is of good height/build, I have been given way more opportunity than most people in this world simply from being born. Combine this with being raised in a Christian family with two loving parents who are still married, and then attending a University and pursuing the dream of professional golf—it has been an incredibly blessed life full of rich experiences. And from these experiences, I have developed an intense idealism that pervades my outlook and perspective on the world.

The point of saying all this is: *I'm biased*. I'll admit it. And ultimately, I can't fully change or eliminate this bias. But even if I could, I wouldn't.... and here's why:

The Science

From examining some of the scientific studies done on the concept of idealism, there were some fascinating (and convincing) results.

One of the most interesting to me was the study[1] done on student-teachers during their first four years of training. The study examined their approach during the first year compared to the second year while focusing on the modification of their beliefs regarding their role as teachers. What they found was that there was a notable shift from an idealistic stance/approach to a more pragmatic view of the teaching experience. If I can paraphrase and summarize it simply: they came into the first year with a heart set on changing the world by impacting the youth they taught, and ended up reverting to a more pragmatic (realistic) view of them assuming the role as teacher and not much else beyond just that.

This isn't a surprising conclusion. In fact, we've all experienced this to some degree. Whether it be when we entered college expecting to be the next "one and done" athlete, or graduating college expecting to be the most coveted recruit for X, Y, or Z company to fight over; hardly ever are we the self-made, self-imposed, divine-gift brought up to bless humanity with our presence. Again, I fall into this category in many ways—e.g.: writing a full-length manuscript, fully expecting it to be picked up and published by a big name publisher…(still working on that).

But, here's the point: we, no, better yet, the world and humanity needs more of this idealism.

In fact, this is the conclusion that the researchers came to at the end of the teaching study mentioned above:

"Contrary to the view that sees primary idealism as an immature, undeveloped position, we contend that idealism and a sense of mission are desired qualities and the shift from "idealism" to "pragmatism" indicates a *regression* and not *progression*." (emphasis added)

Pragmatism is a "regression" from idealism.

From Politics To The Workforce

David Brooks wrote an interesting piece for the NY Times on "The Death of Idealism". In the article, he points out how the political sphere and the recent election in 2016 highlights the complete absence of any form of ideals. He writes:

> "There is no uplift in this race. There is an entire absence, in both campaigns, of any effort to appeal to the higher angels of our nature. There is an assumption, in both campaigns, that we are self-seeking creatures, rather than also loving, serving, hoping, dreaming,

> cooperating creatures. There is a presumption in both candidates that the lowest motivations are the most real."

Caroline Beaton writing for Forbes highlights the fact that most Millennials approach the workforce with the overtly-idealistic idea that they want to (and even can) "make a difference in the world" through their job. Even Caroline wonders whether these individuals will ever survive the realities of life facing the average person, even in America—one of the least "average" societies.

Yet, both Caroline and David come to the same conclusion: we need the younger generations to infuse an optimistic outlook into the currents of culture within our nation and throughout our world. Idealism is what should characterize the younger generation, because pursuing ideals is what leads to human and societal progress.

To quote David on this point, speaking to the political realm, he says:

> "Ironically, one of the tasks for those who succeed the baby boomers is to **restore idealism**. The great challenge of our moment is the crisis of isolation and fragmentation, the need to rebind the fabric of a society that has been torn by selfishness, cynicism, distrust and autonomy.
>
> At some point there will have to be a new vocabulary and a restored anthropology, emphasizing love, friendship, faithfulness, solidarity and neighborliness that pushes people toward connection rather than distrust. Millennials, I think, want to be active in this

rebinding. But inspiration certainly isn't coming from the aging boomers now onstage."

Caroline also ends by affirming this need:

"Idealism doesn't always run counter to reality. In some critical cases, it makes reality. I think the big challenge for millennials isn't to abandon their idealism. It's to keep it even once we have reason not to."

Where's The Balance?

As with anything we try to emphasize, there has to be a healthy balance. If all we ever do is lean into the idealism brewing within Millennials, or those who believe the world needs change and are audacious enough to think they can affect that change, chances are we will never take the practical steps needed to ever arrive at that destination. Ideas are sexy, but until you take action on those ideas they really don't mean anything.

Leon Seltzer, writing in Psychology Today, makes the case for a "cynical idealism," a view that pairs the belief in the impossible (idealism) with the cynical reality of life that sees human motivations as being solely for the promotion of self-interests while recognizing the endless challenges of living on planet Earth. His extensive work on this issue is worth a read as he presents a very balanced and thorough perspective on striking a balance.

How I like to approach this balance follows a slightly different path. Instead of pairing idealism with cynicism—the opposite ends of the spectrum, I prefer to marry idealism with realism—the reality resting in the middle-ish of the spectrum. Yet, the only way this union is successful is by the simple, foundational pursuit of... *discipline*.

The Importance Of Discipline

Changing the world is a **monumental** task. It is so massive a task it can make the staunchest idealist feel defeated. From the realistic point of view, no one person can ever change the world (other than Jesus Christ who arguably did just that). Yet we can leave a lasting impact, but only by working incredibly hard for an incredibly long period of time—which, at the end of the day, takes boatloads of discipline.

Discipline is the one element that can unite Idealism and Realism in holy matrimony. It facilitates the union of two, fairly incompatible perspectives, by daily pushing towards a balance on the see-saw that each side rests on.

Weekends are for dreaming, weekdays are for working. This is an example of a healthy balance in my opinion. Having a big vision is exciting, captivating, and inspiring. But, the only way you ever reach that big vision is if you start putting one foot in front of the other in a practical, yet strategic, pursuit of turning that ideal into a reality.

Ideals are important, but so is realism, and even more-so is discipline. The combination of all three takes a presence and comfortability in the place of tension. Tension, by its nature, is never comfortable. It's not something you simply "get used to". It's always uncomfortable. But, I do believe we can become more comfortable in that place of being uncomfortable—the space of tension between two opposing forces.

Again, I cannot stress enough: the only way this space of

Afterword: The Case For Idealism

tension, this merging of idealism with realism, the only way it is helpful to you and useful to those around you (and the world at large), is if it's lived out and pursued with discipline, the discipline that holds the union together daily.

Dream big, live disciplined.

In summary, here is my point in this lengthy discourse on idealism:

Is idealism a good thing? I believe it is.

Millennials are often branded as "too idealistic". This isn't helpful or fully accurate.

I believe what people really mean when they say this is: Millennials are "too entitled"—and I would agree with that.

Language matters, and the distinction between entitlement and idealism is very important.

Entitlement is the belief that we deserve something that hasn't been earned.

Idealism is the forming and pursuing of ideals - which can often be unrealistic.

… But that's what our generation is for—it's the purpose for this stage of life: to see the opportunities that lay beyond our current grasp. To dream a vision of what the world could be, not what it already is.

Without idealism humans would not progress, norms wouldn't be challenged, and the status quo would never shift.

Yet, there is a balancing reality that needs to be recognized: the need for and importance of realism.

If idealism is the airplane flying at 30,000ft., then realism is the boots on the ground floor doing the dirty work to make things happen.

Realism is the day-by-day, practical, effortful work need to turn the ideals from ideas into reality.

At the end of the day, this takes one vital component — discipline. Saying no to how we feel when it differs from what we know. Saying yes to the work needed in order to get us one step closer to the ideals we hold so dearly. Accepting the reality of our current life and the fact that nothing in life just happens, and if it is meant to be it is up to me.

Discipline leads to ownership. And ownership leads to proper preparation, which leads to more opportunities, and ultimately to optimal performance when those opportunities arise.

So here's to idealism and discipline—a match made in heaven.

---

1. Asher Shkedi, Dina Laron,
    Between idealism and pragmatism: a case study of student teachers' pedagogical development,
    Teaching and Teacher Education,
    Volume 20, Issue 7,
    2004,
    Pages 693-711,
    https://www.sciencedirect.com/science/article/abs/pii/S0742051X04000836

STILL NO HOPE? READ THIS:

HOW TO OVERCOME YOUR SELF-LIMITING BELIEFS

"You're under no obligation to be the same person you were 5 minutes ago." — Alan Watts

"The difficulty lies not so much in developing new ideas as in escaping from old ones." — John Maynard Keynes

"To improve is to change, so to be perfect is to have changed often." — Winston Churchill

---

You can change.

No, I'm serious. You really can.

But why don't you? Why don't *we*?

It's important to know that you're not alone in this problem of change. The struggle to change is a human dilemma that every individual faces to one degree or another. What is shared below will hopefully give you the tools to believe change is possible. The belief that can shift our self-limiting perceptions no matter how ingrained they may be.

One-Sided Thinking

Growing up I had zero creative bones in my body… at least that's what I had thought.

Since I enjoyed the structure, predictability, and formulaic consistency of mathematics, I naturally leaned into where I felt most gifted. I was a "numbers-guy" through and through. In high school, this natural strength continued to show itself as I plowed through college algebra, trigonometry, and calculus, enjoying the challenge every step of the way.

My sister, on the other hand, naturally gravitated toward english and art. She loved creativity and, throughout her high-school years and into college, those creative juices began to blossom into full-bloom. This created a very neat and tidy picture for me, a way to explain our differences away in a logical sense. Simply put: my sister got all the creative genes and I was blessed with none. My perception of myself was contained in a box filled with numbers, logic, and rational thinking, all fueled by the long-standing beliefs I held about the different cards my sister and I were dealt, formed by the repeated thoughts and actions I took all throughout my childhood years.

And then, one day, everything changed…

The more honest version of the story is that, over a period of many days, weeks, and months, unbeknownst to me, everything changed.

What actually transpired over the years was a change in my thoughts and actions that ultimately led to a shifting of my beliefs, and eventually those beliefs created a whole new perception of myself which has unlocked the right side of my brain to function as it can and should, fueling and creating all the work I am blessed to do today.

This is the process of change, and it's actually a pretty simple series of steps.

Sometimes It Happens By Chance

For me it really was an unconscious decision that was made over many months of time. After college, I embarked upon a nearly four-year journey of playing professional golf. In knowing that this pursuit would take me all over the country, I wanted to have a way to keep my friends, family, and fans up to date on how my career was progressing and what I was learning. With the invention of different tools such as Squarespace and Wordpress, creating and maintaining a web presence was now fairly accessible, thus having a website for my golf journey seemed like a perfect fit.

As I created my website and began deciding what would be the best way to keep people in the loop with my career, I figured it could be a fun process to start a blog for tournament results and summaries. Little by little, I began to learn about the world of writing. It began simply, committing to journaling and posting about each tournament I played in. Slowly but surely, as I got a feel for what it took to execute on this vision, I began to start enjoying the process of writing itself!

Me? The numbers guy? The mathematician? The non-creative, only left-side of the brain using dude that grew up thinking there wasn't a creative bone in his body?

This was absolutely novel to me at the time. I was as shocked as anyone else (and probably more so!). But this was the reality I had to come to terms with, and what I came to realize through that process is that the reason why I was never a creative person before was because I never *allowed* myself to be. I never saw (or perceived) myself as someone who was good at creative things, and because I couldn't see it I never believed that I could do it or be it, and this was largely because I had never given myself the chance to try (partly because I had never thought it was worth it).

This massive change, this major shift in who I am—both to myself and to others—all came by chance (or more accurately, by God's leading and directing). This was not an intentional choice. This was not a conscious opening up of myself to my full potential. It was more of a "coming through the back door" and finding myself in a place I had never been before.

But what if I had realized that self-limiting belief sooner? What if I had become aware of that closed perception, the narrow view of myself that prevented me from exercising my full potential? I know it was all perfect in God's timing, but this valuable lesson is one that I want to take forward with me as I continue to grow as a human and I hope you will too.

Admitting The Reality

The first thing we must all admit about change is that **it's hard**. Change is always hard because we always have resistance to change, no matter how "good" that change may be.

"Resistance is proportionate to the size and speed of the change, not to whether the change is a favorable or unfavorable one." — George Leonard

---

Change isn't just hard, it's also impossible without intention. *Positive change never happens by chance.* The only change that results by chance is the development of bad habits, a slide into settling for a life of impulsivity and following the passions and desires of the moment—a lifestyle and mode of living that quickly degenerates into compromise and self-sabotage.

> "We become addicted to our beliefs; we're addicted to our emotions of our past. We see our beliefs as truths, not ideas that we can change." — Dr. Joe Dispenza

---

I'm not going to pretend that change isn't hard, and no one should. But, we must understand and believe that change is possible. Not only is it possible, it can be probable. **The way from possibility to probability is by understanding the process, attaching emotion, and then committing to it for the long-run.** The fruit? Unlimited potential… but seriously.

Understanding The Process

Two of the best books on change are Switch by Chip & Dan Heath, and You Are The Placebo by Dr. Joe Dispenza, and I will be pulling heavily from the latter in what is shared below.

The process of change begins small and builds over time. As we saw in my personal story, it always begins with **thoughts, feelings, and actions**.

> "When you string a succession of thoughts and feelings together so that they ultimately become habituated or automatic, they form an attitude. And since how you think and feel creates a state of being, attitudes are really

just shortened states of being." (You Are The Placebo, 160)

Once we have formed an **attitude** about the situation, ourself, or others around us, we then begin to reinforce that attitude which, over time, becomes a **belief**.

"If you repeat or maintain certain attitudes long enough and you string those attitudes together, that's how you create a belief. A belief is just an extended state of being —essentially, beliefs are thoughts and feelings (attitudes) that you keep thinking and feeling over and over again until you hardwire them in your brain and emotionally condition them into your body." (You Are The Placebo, 161)

Beliefs, as we continue to condition our body and our mind around them, inevitably become our **perception** of the world —the way we view ourselves, others, and our daily lives.

"If you string a group of related beliefs together, they form your perception. So your perception of reality is a sustained state of being that's based on your long-standing beliefs, attitudes, thoughts, and feelings. ... your perceptions—how you subjectively see things—for the most part, become your subconscious and unconscious view of your reality from the past." (You Are The Placebo, 162)

Here's the summary:

Thoughts, Feelings, Actions —> Attitudes —> Beliefs —> Perceptions

How we think, feel, and act on a daily level, over time, turns into our attitudes we carry with us in day-to-day life. As we maintain attitudes over a period of days, weeks, and months, we begin to form beliefs that continue solidifying over years and years of reinforcement. These beliefs are the ideas that make up our perception of reality in all of life, the inherently subjective view we hold on all we say and do.

This is the process of how we form beliefs and why we often think the way we do.

Again, in order to change we must believe that change is possible. How do we believe? First step is always understanding how beliefs are formed. The second step is adding power to the knowledge by attaching our emotions.

> "When you change a belief, you have to start by first accepting that it's possible, then change your level of energy with the heightened emotion you read about earlier, and finally allow your biology to reorganize itself." (You Are The Placebo, 168)

Attaching Emotion

To understand the importance of attaching emotion, let's compare change to love. If you say that you love your spouse or significant other but don't show any emotion attached to that statement it won't be very believable. What helps us know that we are loved are the words and actions filled with emotion that produces the feeling of being loved.

Just as much as we need emotion in love, emotion is required in change.

"But the emotional component is key in this experience; suggestibility isn't just an intellectual process. Many folks can intellectualize being better, but if they can't emotionally embrace the result, then they can't enter into the autonomic nervous system, which is vital because that's the seat of the subconscious programming that's been calling all the shots." (You Are The Placebo, 132)

"By holding a clear and firm intention and heightening our emotional energy, we have to create a new internal experience in our minds and bodies that's greater than the past external experience." (You Are The Placebo, 177)

This is the part of the process that is so often missed in changing our beliefs or perceptions. The power is always found in the emotion. As Chip and Dan Heath frame it in their book Switch, our emotions are similar to an elephant, and our mind or our rational side is the rider of that elephant. In this illustration, the six-ton elephant has unbridled power over the relatively small rider perched atop. This is the importance of recognizing the power of emotions—because we desperately need the elephant's strength and drive in order to create the lasting change we desire.

Emotions are the fuel the can help us start to be the change.

Commitment Produces Change

Like anything worthwhile in life, this is not an overnight process. I didn't wake up one day, magically reinvented as a creative genius (still waiting for that to happen). I did wake up one day and decide to commit to making a step. Then I woke up the next day and kept that commitment to make a step once again. Then, over time, these little steps added up to a large distance covered. I went from viewing myself as a purely analytical, mathematical thinker, to seeing myself as someone filled with creativity, enough to face the daunting task of writing a book, a task I never would have even considered before the journey of change during the years spent competing as a professional golfer.

Commitment cannot be overstated or overvalued in its importance with the process of development in any genre. We must be committed for a long enough period of time in order to see our new attitudes solidify into beliefs and begin forming a new perception of our own abilities and capacity.

> "It takes thinking greater than how they feel—in turn allowing those new thoughts to drive new feelings, which then reinforce those new thoughts—until it becomes a new state of being." (You Are The Placebo, 131)

A new state of being is never accomplished in one day, one week, or even one month. It may be reached in one year, or many years, but it always takes a substantial amount of time, which is why commitment is so necessary.

Practically Speaking

Much of what has been shared is more esoteric in nature, which is often harder to practically apply. The most challenging part of the process is the aspect that we often miss or overlook, the place where the real power lies and the reason why we don't usually experience much success in changing our beliefs about ourself or others: **attaching our emotions**.

The emotions we are most familiar with in daily life are often our survival emotions—the stress hormones that our modern society is so addicted to. These are the emotions of fear, futility, anger, hostility, impatience, pessimism, judgment, anxiety, guilt, shame, lust, worry, doubt, etc. (just to name a few). All of these emotions trigger our fight-or-flight nervous system. These feelings keep us stuck in past emotions and experiences that are reinforced over and over again through these stress responses.

But, as Dr. Joe Dispenza points out in his book, we have the ability to lift our emotions out of the hormonal centers and into the heart. These elevated emotions are only possible if we leave the survival state of being and enter into the thriving state of being, into a selfless mode of existence instead of a selfish state.

To accomplish this, there are two simple tools that we can all practically apply on a daily basis:

1. Gratitude

2. Meditation

Gratitude and appreciation are powerful stimulants for helping us embrace the elevated emotions of love, joy, peace, presence, inspiration, and empowerment. It's an appreciation for what we've been given in life and it teaches us to embody that emotion. As Dr. Dispenza goes on to point out, gratitude is typically experienced after an event has transpired. Thus, having a gratitude practice helps us associate future events with a feeling in the present moment, enabling us to be in a place of receiving instead of acquiring, a state of being instead of having.

Meditation is the tool that enables us to better tap into our subconscious mind—the part of our mind that controls over 95% of our daily lives. It raises our awareness past the immediate stimuli in life that fill up our conscious thoughts, and into the more important processing of the subconscious—where our beliefs and perceptions reside.

> "Meditation takes us from survival to creation; from separation to connection; from imbalance to balance; from emergency mode to growth-and-repair mode; and from the limiting emotions of fear, anger, and sadness to the expansive emotions of joy, freedom, and love. We go from clinging to the known to embracing the unknown." — Dr. Joe Dispenza

---

Wrapping It All Up

Change is hard.

It's hard because we've conditioned ourselves, over time, to perceive ourselves in a certain way. These self-perceptions are fueled by a string of beliefs that have been created by repeated attitudes informed by the thoughts, feelings, and actions of our daily lives.

By understanding how we got here, how these perceptions were formed, we can begin to understand how we can create new perceptions and change our self-limiting beliefs to actually be the change we wish to see.

The real force of change is found in the power of our emotions—the six-ton elephant that our mind rides atop. To create any deep and lasting change, we must attach emotion to our new belief in order to start experiencing that reality in our future by first feeling it in the present.

This is never an overnight process and it will always take a deep and abiding commitment over a prolonged period of time.

The practical tools we can use to help us are 1) gratitude, and 2) meditation.

Through the daily practice of gratitude, we are able to move from the stress emotions found in our hormonal systems to the elevated emotions of our heart.

By practicing meditation, we are able to cross the divide between our conscious and our subconscious minds, tapping into the limitless potential that can be found when we start utilizing the resources found in the part of our brain that controls 95% of our daily lives.

And guess what? We are all capable of that.

We can all be catalysts for the change we wish to be.

You are the placebo.

You don't just hold the key, you are the key.

> "You can't be optimistic about the future until you have survived the crucible of change." — Andrew Grove

---

ABOUT THE AUTHOR

Thane Marcus Ringler is a former professional golfer turned speaker, writer, and development coach living in Denver, CO with his wife Evan.

In his current work, Thane's mission is to help others live and work better. He is passionate about speaking to the journey from the journey, and is striving to empower this generation to take ownership of their lives and never settle for less than they are capable of.

Thane is also the host of The Up & Comers Show, a podcast all about the process of becoming and living with intentionality, while sharing stories from other inspiring up and comers along the way.

To find more on Thane and his work, visit: ThaneMarcus.com

facebook.com/thanemarcus
twitter.com/thanemarcus
instagram.com/thanemarcus

ALSO BY THANE MARCUS RINGLER

From Here To There: A Quarter-Life Perspective On The Path To Mastery

Podcast:

The Up & Comers Show

www.ingramcontent.com/pod-product-compliance
Lightning Source LLC
Chambersburg PA
CBHW070800050426
42452CB00012B/2419